Sunset Liminal

Spring 2015
Volume 1

Poetry Editor

Greg Scheiber

Fiction Editor

Stephen Krzyzanowski

Managing Editor

Kate Gulden

Cover Photo "Through the Crack"
by Kelsey Cochran

Sunset Liminal Press Logo by Chris Balzano

ISBN: 0692419527

ISBN-13: 978-0692419526

Published in Silver Spring, Maryland by Sunset Liminal Press

Letter from the Editor

Dearest Reader,

There are two main groups of people I would thank for making this first issue possible: the poets and the readers. Without these thirteen poets, there would be little work in this issue that all three of us could stand behind and love. And without you, the reader, we would be shuttling off these expressions of the soul into bitterest night. There are few bonds closer than that between a writer and his or her reader. Poets bare themselves to us at their most glorious zeniths and at their lowest nadirs. They take us within places that they are either all too eager to visit or places where they dread every footfall. Poets use words to remind us what humanity is. Like anything, poetry is a spectrum but every point on that spectrum is a moment of transcendence, where the Poet sheds the ability to be judged and in that moment of wordless clarity, asks us to revel, to forgive, to take part in their tears, and to hold their moments of joy as close to our hearts as they hold them to their own.

In this collection, we are asked to soar over New Haven Harbor, to realize the mono no aware of objects and moments left behind by both the deceased and the decayed past, to find and confront the stranger that is ourselves, oftentimes in a strange land, and to share in the nostalgia of memories that we cannot help but to believe we have always been a part of. These thirteen poets have, in their writing, found liminal spaces between relationships to family, friends, and lovers; to the places they are, were, and the places they are going. They have begun to transcend.

I love every one of these poems, and I dearly wish that you, reader, find your own way through these words and love them just as much, if not more, than I do.

Best,

Greg Scheiber
Poetry Editor

Table of Contents

Rachel Martinelli is an undergraduate at Gettysburg College, currently studying Theatre Arts and Writing. Her poetry and artwork has been published in *The Mercury: The Art & Literary Magazine of Gettysburg College.*

Aromantic

I always found it difficult to sleep next to you.

The heat of your chest against my back
and your wet breath on my neck all trapped
beneath that fleece blanket was suffocating,
often unbearable when followed by a round
of frantic kisses and quivering limbs that
lasted longer than I liked and filled
the already thick air with salt and musk.

You wanted to consummate our love.
I just wanted to get off and be done with it.

You were my friend, so for two years I
willed myself to fall into the all-consuming
intensity of love's sun that you write
about in your poetry and that the world
can't seem to keep out of its mythos.

You were Pygmalion, I was your sculpture,
your frigid muse, and though your desire
was flattering to my self-conscious ego,
I could not feel what you felt,

desire what you desired.

You asked the goddess of love to breath warm life into
this ivory body, but my blood calcified at her touch.

Every time you sat me down and told me that I wasn't
doing enough to make you feel loved, that warm smiles
over green tea and quiet conversations over long car rides
were meaningless if they weren't accompanied
by mindless kisses and romantic affirmations,
I would promise to try harder, all the while
wondering why my carnal blood had cooled,
why sex had became the nightly toll to prove
that I was capable of reciprocating the love
I was supposed to feel, a way to alleviate the guilt
I felt for not giving you what you said you needed.

I watched you chip off pieces of yourself and toss
them at my heart's window, attempting to gain entry,
unaware that the glass was two-sided,
that I was standing there the whole time
and just didn't want to let you in.

I searched my alabaster skin for faults, certain a part of me
broke with the collapse of my parent's wedding vows,

that my insides had crumbled into chalky dust ready to seep
through any crevice I didn't fill with kind lies and barren promises.
I thought I needed the hands of another to cover the cracks.

But now I can smile as I claw into my chest, tear out the rib passed down to me from Eve and fling it back at Adam, because I breath easier when all of myself belongs to me.

Pluto

But my disease grew upon me -- for what disease is like Alcohol! Even Pluto began
to experience the effects of my ill temper.

The Black Cat, by Edgar Allen Poe

It was his eyes that captured my devotion.
Cobalt blue and flecked with tenderness, they
caressed my body with translucent ribbons and
tied sinewy, silk bows around my pulsating heart.

We loved in whispers: in whispers and kisses and
those tranquil nights when he would run his fingers
through my obsidian hair and whisper, "My God, Pluto,"
while my throbbing chest vibrated with pleasure.

For years I followed him, a faithful beast hungry for
his affection, addicted to those blue pills that spread
warm deceits through my veins, unaware that my growing
dependency paralleled his swelling intemperance.

I watched gold liquid slosh behind his eyes, watched
them turn a dull, sickly green, felt their malice
slice my body with accusations and tear at my peace of
mind 'til one day I turned away from their scorn.

I did not see the perverse rage my rejection caused until his
bitter knife left me with only one eye to view its savage appetite.
The viscous rust that flowed down my face drained the
gold swamps from his sockets and filled them with horror.
He wailed and begged for my forgiveness, so I gave it.

But my pale bones were stained crimson with dread, and cold
eyes would blaze anew each time I recoiled from their touch.
Yet, I still loved him, my mind blinded by misplaced nostalgia.

I never saw the gallows rise from our bed's frame,
never saw his wretched, hangman's hands,
never saw his noose slide around my brittle neck
'til he pulled the life from my dangling body.

Mike Rebeschi is a man sent back through time to spread tales of adventure and romance, and only ONE lucky lady can accompany him back to the future from whence he came.

Regarding an Affair (and Reading Ezra Pound)

I

The newly woven night drapes
over her body—
and I see the faint light
of a lost sun.

We have numinous visions
that transcend the air
of ancient war,
of its soldiers who saw brighter stars.

And we bathe in Castalia,
our skin holy, and touching;
the tired migration of time,
who keeps watch on love and death
and the ever changing shape of life,
is known to us by the binding truth
of weary kisses—

the sacred embrace of lovers,
the driving force of nature
and the muse of all things—
there is no madness but love

and no love without madness—
our gods strike swift.

I hear a whisper in dim lit darkness,
though I do not know what she said,
I do not want to know.

The desecration of love has commenced
when love's dreams are told—

My genius lies in her,
and all my pretty thoughts are spent:
a worn wick with withering flame
over a wilted flowerbed,
in this season of tangled shadows
beneath the Roman moon.

All our praise for past men,
swallowed by sorrow and passion—
we are slaves to passion—
Za Zen: I have such focus
that I am oblivious.

This ground is firm, yet fertile
like her. And I find myself
only a gardener in the midst
of the deep foliage of forests…
con mi amore, Italia,
kissing my damp chest
like the naked lust of Aphrodite—

her fingertips soft against mine,
mine that are calloused and hardened
by the work of music
and tireless aestheticism.

And when her bare legs
straddle me in the continuing pursuit
of something poetic,
I see her eyes:
dark and glowing with the dew of generosity
and primal stories,
reflecting the shimmer of jealous stars.

II

The willow tree droops in spring,
its leaves sway with the wind
and give me short glimpses
of its wide and imposing trunk,
rising from the ground
like some waking deity
emerging from the depths of
her earthy lair—

the shape of the tree
is like the curvature of your body;
smooth and firm is the bark,
akin to your cold skin
when I run my palms along your hips.
Those little goose bumps tell me

you are waiting for more.

And as I think and start
to come to terms with being sentimental,
I feel the light touch of your lips
on my beard—
your kisses recall a dream:
flying first above New Haven,
in only our skin,
until we flew over a harbor…
her and I dove
into a sea of imagistic snap shots,
until the great white whale himself came
charging from the shroud of deep ocean sadness—

but in slow motion pirouettes
we spiraled out of the water
and into the air—

little droplets spurting off the ends
of our naked, shivering bodies.

Mairead Kress is a first-year at Gettysburg College.

Chest Pains

I'm scared
of the stillness that comes after the storm
because when I was seven,
my teacher told us that
the winds could return
at any second,
and so I must always be careful
when things seem too quiet.

I'm scared
of rollercoasters,
the science of them confuses me
because when I go too fast,
I can't stay on track,
so I wonder how metal
can do what I can't.

I'm scared
of swimming.
Of sinking.
When I was five,
the waves pulled me down,
and I forgot to shout for help
because my mouth
filled with ocean tears
and I added my own to theirs.

I'm scared
of odd numbers because
one always gets left out,
or it just doesn't seem to fit,
and I can't see
the logic of naming something "odd"
and not thinking it
a self-fulfilling prophesy.

I'm scared
of the crack in my bedroom wall —
I could swear gets bigger every day —
I marked in pencil a line and said
"I can worry if it gets to here,"
and I have done that three times,
so I wonder what happens when
I have no more space left to mark.

Jenna Fleming is from Mechanicsburg, Pennsylvania and is a junior at Gettysburg College. She is a History and English double major.

II.

It's taken two years but we've grown roots here,
deep–seated and firm –
fearsome in permanency, strengthened by duality,
twined together far beneath
and beyond these blood–soaked streets.

The first foundations of our tiny black ink architecture
spidering across smooth paper page planes
were built up across shared midnights,
mortared together in bleary-eyed hopefulness,
tested and tried and worn slowly
into some kind of stumbling, bewildered perfection.

You are my lighthouse girl,
and I should be so lucky to see my self reflected
as one of two of a kind –
to hold in my chest one half of a pair
of two bruised purple, fearless, hopeful hearts
brilliant always under one blinding bright moon.

Nicole Byrne suffers from a crippling addiction to poetry and self-medicates with black coffee, avocados, and rock 'n' roll. The treatment does not appear to be working and she hopes it never does. She can be found online at http://www.nicolebyrnepoetry.tumblr.com/.

Just Before 2AM
for Gus

Through the blinds, a shaft
of moonlight finds your back,
then builds a staircase, connecting

your ribs, hip, and thigh: the parts
of your body I touched
with my lips just moments ago.

As you turn to slide your arms
into terrycloth, the stairs fall
away from your skin and break

apart against the wooden door.
On your return, clouds shift
in the sky. Now my eyes must

tread across the memory
of light to find a place for sleep.
In just hours, morning sun

will overwhelm the artful
shadows and leave our bodies

bare. When we wake, I'll close

my eyes, bury myself as long
as I can against the brightness.
But you, as always, will rise

to meet it, shrugging off the night.

In Your Bed

Every capillary in the body constricts
to cut off the tributaries that carry speech
through the throat, and the tongue presses
against the teeth in hopes of pushing out
phonemes, and fingers with freshly-filed
nails twitch and dig enough to leave behind
half-moon marks long after muscles have pulled
away the hands and heat rises from the cavity
that keeps the quickening heart as quiet as possible
and dissipates from the tips of reddening ears,
and the diaphragm feels stiffer and it requires
conscious effort to expand each lung, and then
when all blood vessels are on the verge of bursting,
and the hands stop clenching in time with heart
palpitations, and the phonetic lessons memorized
in childhood return, and vocal cords vibrate to cause
the mouth to open wide enough to let lips protest against
the parting of lips, organs contract and erupt
like a plastic bottle squeezed
tight in a rejected fist
with exactly
the right
amount
of air
to say

No.

Elegy for My Grandfather

Death bleached his Torch Red Corvette
in my mother's dreams, the car as white
as her face when she woke at night, wailing
He knows we sold his house. Her voice echoed
through the kitchen and pooled
atop a crumpled flyer from the estate sale.

For my grandmother, his death was a dream.
She'd place an extra plate on the dinner table,
set daily reminders for his medication,
and clipped his favorite comics and columns
from the Sunday paper. His name wheezed
from her lips when she dozed.

I could not dream of him until years
later, his presence in my sleep
not confused as an act of bleeding
grief—a half-assed attempt to bring him back—
but a ringer of memory struck by a game
of horseshoes I played earlier that day.

Liz Williams lives in Pittsburgh, PA, where she enjoys vegetarian cooking, Russian novels, and bike rides along the Monongahela River. She was an English major with a writing concentration at Gettysburg College and now works in donor relations at Carnegie Mellon University.

Space

Gold hardened leaf—
cracked, thin with dry-bone veins
in black along its back—
descends, drops lightly on its ordinary path
to brown below.
Its new space among the other dead
jars this leaf, as does mine:
my new and jagged loft with
corners fresh and radiator yawning.

Here I am within my ordinary plot,
with giddy job and
golden boy awaiting
just outside. Pumpkin,
fresh from oven's mouth
fills this space, and all around me
floats this life's menagerie of objects:
my own collected things
all uncertain they should settle.

What's in a room but bulbs and boards?
Surely there is nothing more.
But I linger above,

like a puffed mylar balloon
puckered in its half-used state,
suspended just above the floor
and not quite ready to commit,
either up or down—
to gravity or
the air.

Sangria berries

These berries, wine–infused, are much too plump
for me to stab, their pregnant cores too soft
to meet pale cleaver teeth or muscled tongue.
Discarded at the bottom of the jug,
their mother liquid long ago dispensed,

they clump together, now exposed. Six days
ago I measured out in cups and bowls
proportions said to magnetize and hold
a circle: arms extending toward the center,
glasses raised to loosen thirsty lips.

Sweet sangria: drunk, absorbed, and dripped
out in the sewers, in so many sewers.
I am spilled out now across the skylines
and the highways, in endless envy of the
berries–so compact, condensed, and close.

Fountain at the Point

The current is magnetic:
Not like the heave and pull of undertow
in rivers' and oceans' pulsing flow,
but a vertical surge splintering the air,
a two-hand touch on the shadow of a cloud
then droplets hurtled down to the ground,
spilling like pennies over the platform's edge.

This fountain, in its droning rhythm,
draws the bodies in along its spokes:
Suited men with paws on sandwiches
with too-white bread,
and daisy girls cartwheeling along the cement,
pigtails picking up dust as mothers lament
to each other and to themselves.

We watch its dance, convinced this is nature before us
and not another man-made attempt
to entertain and to change our ideas
of what we need and how to 'be.'
It is serene—narcotic—and as long as we stare,
the smoke-stacks behind us will float away like dreams,
like silly old stories for another day.

When he isn't doing (almost) anything else, you'll find **Gordon Moore** writing – generally poetry, and generally as deep into the night as work or the world permits him. He's also generally terrible at working his way through the trove of notebooks and pens he's picked up over the years, and occasionally enjoys standing on a stage so he can fumble up a reading of something he's written. That being said, if you've got words worth sharing, he'd like to read them.

Violet

Standing in the wheat fields,
waiting for the storm.

God couldn't tell you
what color my eyes are now.

The revolving winds
on the horizon,
but all I feel is the
rising heat
and the tempered flush
and the way her words run rampant
over my jacket, through my hair,
the way they work to etch themselves
upon my skin.

These brands, this fire, though;
it isn't enough to sear.
Runes and shapes,
they're all peeled off

of someone else's dreamscapes,
and I am exhausted with all the days
I've lived here, unaffected.

So to say,
before the hurricane,
that the first waves of this moment
are all magic, and still submerged
in disappointment,
I'm sure I sound the ass you knew me as.
I'm sorry.
It can't be any fun,
hearing me this way.

It can't be any fun,
loving someone
who loves to drown in dreams.

But this is the arc I was made for;
this is the way I'm going to have to be.

When the eye is upon me,
when the chaff, and the town around
ascend,
when the ground gives way
and the ground gives way
and the violet of the world below
peers through,
will I be standing before you?

Lumps

If you pressed me to it –
and you are,
damn you,
the way that only you would,
drinking swill and strange concoctions out here,
well beyond the marker between days –

well,
I'd try to laugh it off afterwards,
do my best to ignore your stare,
but I'd tell you of the room where I lost
a few years.

Couch, crumpled,
black iron bars at each end,
creaking. And
something wriggling
inside.

A cheap red tear of fabric
covering the window,
and nothing on the floor, save
the boxes in the corner,
joining floor to ceiling.
At least one of them has things in it
I'd be better to forget.

And I would tell you that there was a screen upon the wall
that pulled me in, spoke magic,
sent effervescent, ultraviolet light
over everything, and
if it wasn't on, neither was I.

I'd tell you I remember
the way the curves of that black futon held me,
the things it told me in the dark
as I fell, weightless,
from dream to dying dream.

and
I'd tell you that every bed since has been
lifeless,
and that there are days when I stand, distracted,
and doing my best not to run when
I see it, descending,
blotting out sun.

Victoria Reynolds is currently an English Literature major at Gettysburg College, located in Pennsylvania. She is twenty-two years old and has never broken a bone, and never wishes to. She was born in Philadelphia, Pennsylvania during a blizzard that nearly kept her father from witnessing her birth, even though he drove a snow plow.

Birth Bouquet

I was your baby's breath,
fleeting softness,
skin a touch of milky white,
before I had my teeth.
The gristle in your breast
may have hardened even then,
and not later in the years
when I pressed fingers into ears
to avoid the bite of your marriage gone sour.
Your mastectomy
will be my lobotomy,
pulling away half a childhood
I had never even touched.
Enamel had just blossomed
through red beds
of my mouth crying "Mama,"
as your second baby girl
– a sister for me –
turned in the wheel of your womb,
a catalyst for cancer,
the doctors told us.
Hormones hastened

the disease that might have devoured
you late in your life.
If you had lived
until your ripest years,
perhaps you could have cradled
a grandchild,
a new breath from one of your buds,
but you are the one thing
I cannot give to my children.

Lamprocapnos spectabilis

You were born, years ago, in August,
five months after spring cycles back,
and our favorite flower was the bleeding heart,
the "lady-in-a-bath,"
with its arching sprays
of heart-shaped flowers
unable to pick themselves up,
like your neck and head in the last days.
It was hard for you
to lift your head up,
a heavy stem tipped forward
towards the earth we would bury you in.
It was spring ephemeral,
like you, with your withering leaves.
You mimicked it and
died down to your fibrous roots
as soon as summer fell away.
You disappeared by the close of the year
with snow falling onto our wooden floors
and a gold and ruby coverlet
pulled up over what was left of you.
I still dig in the garden,
hoping to find a root,
a rhizome, one bulb left of you.

Nicole Yackley graduated summa cum laude from the University of Georgia with a BA in English, a concentration in Creative Writing, and a minor in Studio Art. More of her writing can be found at http://www.whirlsofwords.tumblr.com/.

Holes in the knees of my jeans

The cover of the sky is torn, and I
can see the stuffing poking through.
But not on you. Every corner
sewn up tighter than an honest alibi.
A reasonable excuse: all ways out
with no way in. Come, while I have you
in shirtsleeves—let's lean out of windows
so I can see whose ragged claws
cause closed blinds. Come, while I have
you in shirtsleeves—let's put on layers
together, so I'll know them next time.
I want to learn why you reach for a blank face
when you get dressed in the morning.

Emily Pierce is from Connecticut, and is currently a Theatre Arts major with a minor in Music at Gettysburg College. She was an editor for the 2015 edition of the college's literary magazine *The Mercury*. In her boundless spare time, she also enjoys writing songs and plays.

Guy Fawkes Day

twenty seconds

you don't blink
(or at least, not as much as I do)

your eyes are closer together than mine
and all I really want to do is memorize your face
in this moment when I am permitted,
but this will do
and I will keep your shade of blue
as a souvenir

thirty seconds

I thank myself briefly for remembering my sweater
my naked shoulders are not ready for your hands
perhaps they will never learn what that is like

still
back to blue and something much better than sun lamps
I sense, I savor, I somehow convince myself this could be real

forty-five seconds

I want to apologize—I always do—but

to hold and be held

to breathe you in, even a little

my chest is a featherweight rock,

a skipping stone

you have never known me to be so at ease

and I can't bring myself to worry about whether you will know it
        again

because this moment takes your shape

and brings me close to a tempo of peace

and I beg forgiveness again

as I now fail to keep time

but certainly, it should last much longer

I freeze

even in the face of your warmth, my glow

lack of experience but surplus in passion frightens me,

but you know what to say—you always do—

and I will not accept your apologies because you've already given me
        so much,

even if you don't know it

there is a box of treasures in my heart and it has your name etched
        onto the side

do not apologize for making me melt

I had wondered about your lips

to say I like how they feel would be a criminal dilution

again

only slightly aware of my own incompetence

I am pleased to lose myself
again

one chaste, one more scarlet
again
this is for the audience, I know, I know, I know
but I forget and take it for myself

again

sixteen days are left
and then you will never have to kiss me again

still
this precious keepsake will remain in my treasure-box
long after the fireworks are over

Maude Mowbray is a determined twenty–something from the South Eastern United States. She is currently putting her recently earned BA in English to good use by working on a seemingly endless amount of cover letters and applications. Maude collects road maps and hopes to one day own a little roadside restaurant.

Long–Term Goals

I plan to write a poem in every state,
and leave each in another,
perhaps nailed to a tree or hidden
in a hotel Bible in hope
that when you someday day seek
answers in either Mother or Father
you will find me again.

But you are more likely
to seek something stronger,
      like gin
or women bolder than I,
and these scribbled confessions
are fated to fade.
Dust to dust,
and ashes to ashes.

Lesseps' Lament

I've been slipping soliloquies beneath my bed sheets lately,
and whispering sweet sonnets and iambs and prose poems of prayer,
as if this over-emotional padding might keep me half as warm
as you once did.

I've been praying that this long aside might finally be
interrupted by a supporting cast of characters,
(who instead seem to have fallen out
of the Author's consciousness in favor of this
painful poetic musing, which will act as little
more than over-enunciated audition
material for hopeless romantic
rejects in years to come).

I've been dreaming of my monologues
becoming our dialogues in more
fully developed scenes, in something less
meta and more—

I've been mourning, my love.

In the Absence of Snow

As a child, I was deprived of that
annual accumulation of frozen precipitation
you say a Daughter of the North is due.
    (We moved to a Land of Heat and
    Sun and Moonshine when I was four.)
Instead of pining for sugar-plum-coated fantasies of
iconic White Christmases, I learned to romanticize the glow
of brightly colored bobbles and their reflections in the raindrops
rolling down the other side of thick glass windows.

I have begun to crave the heavy, damp taste of the days in late July
    when the rumbling
stomachs of the overhead clouds would call out every afternoon
    between supper and lunch,
compelling each reluctant child to crawl out of the cool,
    chlorinated water
to seek shelter beneath the covered patio at the neighborhood pool,
where we would wait
    (impatiently)
for fifteen minutes
of heavenly
silence
to finally signal our safe return to the shallows.

I miss spending similar storms sitting in screened-in porches
in once-white plastic chairs
    (always dusted yellow)
waiting for each slow clap's increase until

the thunderous applause encouraged an encore
of a downpour that cleansed the brick and wood
and left pollen-lined puddles swirling
like galaxies of sickly stars on the deck.

I was deprived of great snowstorms as a child.
Having returned to this Land of Kin and Cold,
I am left not knowing what to make of this empty dreamscape
that blurs lines of reality between each once familiar path and object,
making them nothing more than vague outlines,
of the same kind and color as unfinished images
in an unused paint-by-numbers book.

I never learned how to fill in these empty spaces
and despite having ample imaginaries to draw on,
every hue of blue on my imaginary artist's pallet fades
to your eyes, purer and bluer
than the city's sky could ever hope to be,
more the blue of mountain air or hidden stream,
every yellow shines golden as your fair hair
every red becomes your lips grazing mine
until each color becomes at once over-
mixed, indistinguishable, and over-worked.
Every color an amalgamation of
you
and quite unsuitable for any numbered book.

Sam Orndorff writes prose, poetry, and polemic. He teaches English in South Korea while working on a novel. Look for his work in *riverSedge* and *Gravel.* Smooch him at smoochjazz@gmail.com.

Imaginary Line Patrol

~~Jungle~~
Rainforest
They
Two Legs
~~National Security~~

Grave
Hill
Holding
Skull
Carcass
Doll
Sun

Free
~~Illegal~~
Trade

~~Hand~~
Traffic
Rhetoric
~~Visible~~

Insane

Inspector

Imprint

~~Human Nature~~

Carcinogenesis

~~Aspects:~~

Frozen

~~Destiny~~

Roots

Anesthetic

Blonde

Yawn

Cargo

~~Access~~

Access

Revolutionary

Likeness

Horizon

~~Liberate~~

Perdido

Qué

Paso

Nothing

New

Kiss

Air

Overpass

Feel
~~Present~~
Paved

~~Complementary~~
Stereotypes
Tuned
~~Tomorrow~~

The–Not
–Dead
–Dance

~~In Two~~
Places
~~At once~~

Emily Francisco is currently pursuing two masters degrees in Art History and Museum Studies at Syracuse University, where she works as a Teaching Assistant for the Department of Art & Music Histories. She received her BA in Art History and English with a Writing Concentration from Gettysburg College, where she completed the manuscript for her short poetry collection *Artemisia in the Metro*, which she hopes to continue working on and publish in the future. Her work has been published in the *Cupola*, the *Mercury*, and the *Helix*, and she has been awarded two Marion Zulauf Poetry Prizes for her poems "Connection" (2012) and "Lessons in Tourism" (2014). She is also one of the co-founders of the Live Poet's Society, an independent literary club and workshop located in Gettysburg, PA.

On Defeat

After Laocoon and his Sons, *the original Greek sculpture possessed by the Vatican Museums.*

Is this death,

            the gasp of fear
      in the father's eyes,

the pulse of the jugular
            and abdominal muscles

      arching back, into no plane at all,

empty space caressing the limbs
            of marble as he falls backward

      (sculpture in the round)—

all tangled limbs, no bed

of violet porphyry,

(the stone of emperors)

veined with ropes of white
            to catch his body as the serpent

    throws him into the void.

The boys, barely frowning,
            bear furrowed brows, fearful lips,

    yet no exclamation of agony,

not a gasp of pain
            nor the grimace of fear

    carved into their cheeks,

only surprise, then acceptance
            while Apollo's pet thrashes his ivory

    jaw into their father's hip.

It is as if this is no death at all,
            only a dream, pictorial representation

    as it is—like they know they are but a story,

and assume their descent

into the negative space of myth,

that blank unoccupied hollow

between object and life,
                like their father before them

        falling into the bleak air

with purpose, only
                calmly sacrificing physical lives

        in favor of fictional ones,

suffocating the limbs of history
                in the trembling scales

        of an undulant monster.

Driving Past Dead Sunflowers in October

Crippled and brown, as if burnt,
shriveled from weeks of thirst,

yet still they are as tall
as scarecrows, thin roots

staking the dirt with some unfeeble
strength, heads sagging

in a downward glance
as if to make sure they are still there,

the legumes that tie them to the earth,
gossamer umbilical threads yet to be cut.

Though I know this is how it is here,
this is how the harvest is done

(by killing the golden crop in late summer),
still I feel an internal companionship

with these bodies as they wait,
solemnly, for the black gems

to slip from their mouths,
seeds tokens of another year gone,

one year closer to the inevitable turning
of the field to fallow.

On Language

It's the exhaustion of words
that kills the body,

every salt -tipped consonant
and bulleted vowel

a struggle to wield,
weapons given to an ignorant youth,

the gun of syntax more
likely to be turned inward

than outward to an opponent.
Lessons can only do so much —

walking to the immigration office,
my brain mixes translations

together like a stew of leftovers,
every Italian syllable a soft, mushy carrot

and every French article
a bone of frozen *poulet,*

the flavors slipping together
in a broth so murky

that the thought of conversing —
forming sentences, making dialogue —

is repulsive, nauseating to my weak senses,
fragile in their new environment.

One sip of the broth,
and it is already rising in my throat

like bile, the phrases coming out
in jumbled fragments, chunks

of knowledge I knew yesterday
in a classroom of seven,

now expelled from my esophagus
in frantic sprays of, "Est –ce que vous parli —

parli inglese?"
Drowning in the prose,

lost on the way to the *questura*,
my romantic *Firenze* disappears,

and I see only a city of acrid yellow
and sordidly brown buildings,

monotonous shapes taunting
my American eyes with the blunt honesty

of reality, that I am alone
in this place called *Italia*,

mute and stranded
as a migrant pigeon,

so eager to flock to a new metropolis,
flying abroad to seek fresh

pickings from the rabble,
to feel foreign rain

graze my wings as I bathe,
but instead, I find myself desperately

nipping at the shoes of strangers,
hoping, begging, pleading for a single

crumb of guidance
for my foreign tongue to swallow.

Enjoyed *Sunset Liminal?* Be on the lookout for Volume II, coming out this Fall!

If you want to have a shot at having your work featured in the next issue of *Sunset Liminal,* e-mail one prose piece or up to five poems as .doc or .docx attachments to <u>sunsetliminal@gmail.com</u> with either "Poetry Submissions" or "Fiction Submissions" in the subject line.

If you're interested in learning more, like us on Facebook and follow us on Tumblr and Twitter.

http://www.facebook.com/sunsetliminalpress/
http://www.sunsetliminal.tumblr.com/
https://twitter.com/SunsetLiminal/

www.ingramcontent.com/pod-product-compliance
Lightning Source LLC
Chambersburg PA
CBHW050949030426
42339CB00007B/353